to: my daughter's

from: Mon

date: Oct 2015

forget *love,* I'd rather fall in *chocolate*

ARTWORK BY
·LINDA MARON·

HARVEST HOUSE PUBLISHERS

EUGENE, OREGON

FORGET LOVE, I'D RATHER FALL IN CHOCOLATE

Text Copyright © 2009 by Harvest House Publishers
Artwork Copyright © by Linda Maron
Published by Harvest House Publishers
Eugene, Oregon 97402
www.harvesthousepublishers.com

ISBN 978-0-7369-2606-5

Design and production by Rachel Lyn Closs

Printed in China
13 14 15 / LP / 10 9 8 7 6 5 4 3

There's nothing better than a good friend,
except a good friend with chocolate.

· Linda Grayson ·

In my mouth the chocolate broke at first like gravel into many separate, disagreeable bits. I began to wonder if I could swallow them. Then they grew soft, and melted voluptuously into a warm stream down my throat.

The little doctor came bustling up, his proudly displayed alpenstock tucked under one short arm.

"Here! Wait, wait!" he cried. "Never eat chocolate without bread, young lady! Very bad for your interior, very bad..."

And in two minutes my mouth was full of fresh bread, and melting chocolate, and as we sat gingerly... we peered shyly and silently at each other and smiled and chewed at one of the most satisfying things I have ever eaten.

• M.F.K. Fisher •
LONG AGO IN FRANCE

chocolate

is ground from the beans of

HAPPINESS.

• Alexis F. Hope •

Always

serve too much hot fudge
sauce on hot fudge sundaes.
It makes people overjoyed,
and puts them in your debt.

· Judith Olney ·

the Perfect Match

A great couple is a great couple. Forget Bogie and McCall, I'm talking about the delicious matches made by combining other ingredients with chocolate. We all know chocolate on its own is perfectly divine, but now and then it likes to lend its brilliance to other foods...

And the results are stunning:

- Chocolate and nuts
- Chocolate-covered espresso beans
- Chocolate with chili peppers
- Chocolate and mint (think ice cream!)
- Chocolate-covered pretzels
- Chocolate and fruit
  (cherries, strawberries, even blueberries)
- Chocolate with caramel or nougat
- Chocolate with bacon! (Yes, it exists)
- Chocolate with peanut butter
- Chocolate and marshmallows

And WHO DOESN'T LOVE A MOCHA LATTE AT THEIR FAVORITE BEANERY?

The closer you get to a pure chocolate liquor
(the chocolate essence ground from roasted cacao bean
the purer it is, the more satisfying it is, the safer it is,
and the healthier it is.

• Arnold Ismach •
THE DARKER SIDE OF CHOCOLATE

aste and see that the LORD is good.

· THE BOOK OF PSALMS ·

THE BEST CHOCOLATES
engage all of our senses.
Great chocolates balance all of the
sense elements in a harmonious whole
that is greater than the sum of the
individual parts.

• Clay Gordon •
DISCOVER CHOCOLATE

Caramels are only a fad.
Chocolate is a
permanent thing.

• Milton S. Hershey •

Chocolate for Every Mood Cookies

Feel reflective? Feel cheery? Feed your every whim with chocolate. By using cake mixes, one can invent the perfect chocolate cookie to suit any preference and any mood. The freedom to be creative might change a down day into a decadent one.

ingredients

1 box of cake mix:
chocolate, chocolate fudge,
German chocolate...
endless possibilities

2 eggs

2 teaspoons water
(add a dash more if you add a package
of pudding—see opposite page)

⅓ cup vegetable oil

Drop or two of vanilla

optional items

• 1 package of unprepared instant pudding in any flavor (double up on the chocolate!)

• Nuts or chips (try butterscotch, cinnamon, peanut butter, or chocolate)

[directions]

Preheat oven for 325 to 350°. Mix all ingredients together. Drop mixture by the spoonful onto a greased cookie sheet and bake for 10 minutes. They should be soft when you take them out of the oven. Move cookies to a cooling rack. Makes 1½ to 2 dozen cookies.

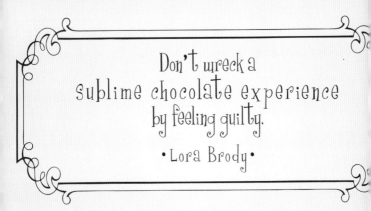

Don't wreck a
sublime chocolate experience
by feeling guilty.

• Lora Brody •

Life is uncertain.
Eat dessert first.

· Ernestine Ulmer ·

Monsieur turned to his wife and said happily, "What a pleasure, to watch a child eat her first souffle!" She inclined her head in regal agreement. He winked at me.

"Close your eyes," he commanded as I took the first bite. I did, and my mouth closed over the hot, fragrant air only to have it disappear at once. But the flavor stayed behind, the chocolate reverberating from one side of my mouth to the other. I took another bite, hoping that I could make the texture last a little. I couldn't, but I kept trying.

• Ruth Reichl •
TENDER AT THE BONE

IT'S NOT THAT
CHOCOLATES ARE
A SUBSTITUTE FOR LOVE...

love
is a substitute for chocolate.

• Miranda Ingram •

A Chocolate Lover's Guide to Chocolat

THE BETTER YOU KNOW YOUR
chocolate,
THE MORE JOY YOU'LL GET OUT OF IT.

- **Unsweetened chocolate:** The basic chocolate from which all other products are made.

- **Semisweet chocolate:** Unsweetened chocolate with sugar, additional cocoa butter, and flavorings added.

- **Sweet cooking chocolate:** Similar to semisweet chocolate, but with a higher proportion of sugar.

•**Milk chocolate:** Sweet chocolate with milk added and packaged in various-sized bars.

•**Almond bark:** Vanilla-flavored candy coating made with vegetable fats instead of cocoa butter, with coloring and flavorings added.

•**Unsweetened cocoa:** Pure chocolate with most of the cocoa butter removed and ground into powder form.

•**Chocolate syrup:** Combination of cocoa, corn syrup, and flavoring.

TAKEN FROM:
PILLSBURY'S CHOCOLATE LOVERS II COOKBOOK

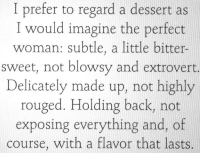

I prefer to regard a dessert as I would imagine the perfect woman: subtle, a little bitter-sweet, not blowsy and extrovert. Delicately made up, not highly rouged. Holding back, not exposing everything and, of course, with a flavor that lasts.

• Graham Kerr •

Strength is the capacity to
BREAK A CHOCOLATE BAR INTO FOUR PIECES
with your bare hands—and then
eat just one of the pieces.

• Judith Viorst •

Biochemically, love
is just like eating large
amounts of chocolate.

• John Milton •

Just looking at the almond cake is almost enough satisfaction, but instead we split one of the crisp cannoli lined with chocolate and heavenly, creamy ricotta. No harm done; we're planning to walk for the rest of the afternoon.

• Frances Mayes •
BELLA TUSCANY

Listen, listen to me, and eat what is good, and your soul will delight in the richest of fare.

• The Book of Isaiah •

chocolate soda

ingredients

❧

2 large scoops fudge
ice cream (or 1 scoop vanilla
& 1 scoop chocolate)

3 tablespoons chocolate sauce

cola or club soda

whipped topping

directions

Place 1 scoop of ice cream at the bottom of a large drinking glass or old-fashioned soda glass. Add chocolate sauce. Fill the glass with cola or with the club soda. Leave about 2 inches at the top and then add the second scoop of ice cream. If desired, top it off with the whipped topping.

Other things ARE JUST FOOD. But chocolate's chocolat

• Patrick Skene Catling •

YOU WANT TO SAVOR THE MOMENT,
to let your jaw relax and relish the sensation
of the smooth creamy chocolate against
the hard, crunchy candy.

But you can't.

The thought of the next mouthful is too powerful.
Quickly, you swallow; and then, without
thinking, you reach for more.

• Joel Glenn Brenner •
THE EMPERORS OF CHOCOLATE

The best chocolates
ENGAGE ALL OF OUR SENSES.
Great chocolates balance all of the sense
elements in a harmonious whole that is
greater than the sum of the
individual parts.

• Clay Gordon •
DISCOVER CHOCOLATE

Oh, divine chocolate!

ey grind thee kneeling, Beat thee with hands praying,

And drink thee with eyes to heaven.

• Marco Antonio Orellana •

Poor beauty! She gazed and gazed through her tears, and so mounted the stairs sorrowfully back to her own chamber. On reaching it she felt herself oppressed with sleepiness, for she had passed the night without undressing, and, moreover, for a month past her sleep had been broken and haunted with terrors. So, having nothing better to do, she went to bed, and was nestling down in the perfumed sheets when her eyes fell on the little table by the bedside.

Someone had set **a cup of hot chocolate** there, and half asleep, she reached out her hand for it and drank it; whereupon her eyes closed and she fell into a delicious slumber, such as she had not known since the day when her father brought home the fatal rose.

• Sir Arthur Quiller-Couch •
"BEAUTY AND THE BEAST"

A WHIRLWIND
romance

A woman in love might talk in terms of being

"over the moon"

for a guy, but if a girl has her compass set to
chocolate, her heart can travel to even

tastier destinations.

HERSHEY'S CHOCOLATE WORLD
Hershey, Pennsylvania

A GOURMET CHOCOLATE TOUR
in San Francisco, Chicago, or New York

THE HOME OF NESTLÉ IN SWITZERLAND
there's nothing neutral about their chocolate selection

ADVENTURE IN AFRICA
the world's leading producer of cocoa beans

CAN'T TRAVEL?
Visit the Willy Wonka World online at www.WillyWonka.com.

The superiority of chocolate
both for health and
nourishment will soon give
it the same preference over
tea and coffee in America
which it has in Spain.

• Thomas Jefferson•

If you get melted chocolate
all over your hands,
you're eating it too slowly.

• Author Unknown •

Dear Kermit:

Mother went off for three days to New York and Mame and Quentin took instant advantage of her absence to fall sick. Quentin's sickness was surely due to a riot in candy and ice-cream with chocolate sauce. He was a very sad bunny next morning and spent a couple of days in bed.

• Theodore Roosevelt •
THEODORE ROOSEVELT'S LETTERS
TO HIS CHILDREN

"Nearly eleven o'clock,"
said Pooh happily.
"You're just in time for a
little smackerel of something."

• A.A. Milne •
THE HOUSE AT POOH CORNER

mocha latte cookies

ingredients

1¼ cups all-purpose flour

⅛ teaspoon salt

½ teaspoon baking powder

⅛ teaspoon ground cinnamon

½ cup unsalted butter, softened

⅓ cup dark brown sugar

⅓ cup granulated sugar

1 large egg

1½ teaspoons instant espresso powder

1 teaspoon vanilla extract

1 cup miniature semisweet chocolate chips

½ cup miniature cinnamon chips

directions

Preheat oven to 375°.
In a bowl, stir together flour, salt,
baking powder, and cinnamon. In another bowl,
cream together butter and sugars until combined.
Mix in the egg. In a separate bowl, stir espresso powder
with vanilla until dissolved and then add into butter
mixture until combined. Gradually stir in flour mixture
til blended. Stir in chips. Cover and refrigerate dough for
one hour. Lightly butter two large baking sheets. Drop
spoonfuls of dough onto sheets about 2 inches apart.
Bake one sheet at a time, for 9 to 14 minutes, or
until cookies are lightly browned. When done,
move sheet to a wire rack and cool for the first
couple of minutes, then transfer cookies to a
wire rack to cool completely.
Makes 2 dozen.

chocolate.

The beverage chocolate made by dissolving chocolate in hot milk is a wholesome, agreeable drink, when used moderately. Unlike tea and coffee, it has valuable food properties in addition to being an excitant of the nervous system.

nutritious food

The uses of chocolate in making confectionery, pastry, puddings, and ice cream are numerous and well known. It is rich in fat, the proportion being, on an average, 48.7 per cent, and is therefore a nutritious food.

• THE WORLD BOOK, 1926 •

Never mind about 1066 William the Conqueror, 1087 William the Second. Such things are not going to affect one's life...but 1932 the Mars Bar and 1936 Maltesers, and 1937 the Kit Kat—these dates are milestones in history and should be seared into the memory of every child in the country.

• Roald Dahl •

Life without chocolate is
life lacking something important.

• Marcia Colman Morton
& Frederic Morton •

chocolate is the only aromatherapy I need.

• Jasmine Heiler •

Fudge is…
  a noun,
  a verb,
  an interjection,
  and delicious!

• Jessi Lane Adams •

"I expect that's my cocoa," said Paddington importantly. "The steward always brings me some before I go to bed."

The others exchanged glances as the door opened and a man in a white coat entered carrying a tray laden with a large jug of steaming hot liquid.

"This is the life," exclaimed Mr. Brown.

the life..."

...Paddington nodded happily as the steward sorted out some extra mugs and began to pour. He was keen on cocoa at the best of times, especially ship's cocoa which somehow always had a taste of its own... He eyed the jug from behind a cloud of rich, brown steam. "There's only one thing nicer, Mr. Brown," he announced amid general agreement. "And that's *two* cups!"

• Michael Bond •
PADDINGTON AT WORK

When Mr. Nilsson had emptied his cup,
he turned it upside down and put it on his head.
When Pippi saw that, she did the same, but as she
had not drunk quite all her chocolate a little stream
ran down her forehead and over her nose. She
caught it with her tongue and lapped it all up....

"Waste not, want not," she said.

• Astrid Lindgren •
PIPPI LONGSTOCKING

Chocolate causes certain endocrine glands to secrete hormones that affect your feelings and behavior by making you happy. Therefore, it counteracts depression, in turn reducing the stress of depression. Your stress-free life helps you maintain a youthful disposition, both physically and mentally. So, eat lots of chocolate!

• Elaine Sherman •
BOOK OF DIVINE INDULGENCES

S t r e s s e d
spelled backwards is
d e s s e r t s.
Coincidence?
I think not!

• Author Unknown •

Emilie's Triple Chocolate Fudge Cake

ingredients

1 small package chocolate pudding (not instant)

1 box chocolate cake mix

½ cup semisweet chocolate pieces

½ cup chopped nuts

Whipped cream

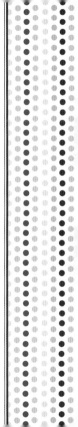

directions

Cook pudding as directed on the package and blend dry cake mix into hot pudding.

Pour mixture into prepared oblong pan (13 x 9 x 2 inches) and sprinkle with chocolate pieces and nuts. Bake 30 to 35 minutes at 350°. Cool 5 minutes; cut into 2-inch squares. Top with whipped cream.

• Emilie Barnes •
THE TWELVE TEAS OF CHRISTMAS

chocolate

is an antidepressant, which is especially useful as you start to gain weight.

• Jason Love •

MAKE A LIST OF IMPORTANT THINGS
TO DO TODAY.
At the top of your list, put

" *eat chocolate* ."
NOW, you'll get at least
one thing done today.

• Gina Hayes •

CHOCOLATE IS A PERFECT FOOD,
as wholesome as it is delicious,
a beneficent restorer of exhausted
power. It is the best friend of those
engaged in literary pursuits.

• Baron Justus von Liebig •
German chemist (1803–1873)

Chocolate

remedies adversity.

· Jareb Teague ·

I HAVE THIS THEORY THAT

chocolate slows down the aging process...

IT MAY NOT BE TRUE,
BUT DO I DARE TAKE THE CHANCE?

• Author Unknown •

Chocolate...

is the Big Magoo. It is The Ingredient. It is the Fred Astaire of the cookie world. The Eiffel Tower of baking. The Cole Porter of oven harmonies. Chocolate delights the palate, stirs the emotions, and separates the truly sophisticated gourmet from those who eat to live.

• Bob and Suzanne Stat •
THE COMPLETE CHOCOLATE CHIP
COOKIE BOOK